MW00979167

First Printing: 2018
ISBN 978-0-359-11785-7

Cannabis Strain Journal
The Moon Phases Me
Talent, Oregon 97540

A @TheMoonPhasesMe Journal
MoonPhasesMe@Yahoo.com

Cannabis Strain Journal

A @TheMoonPhasesMe Journal
by Untitled Cannabis Project

Cannabis is a unique medication. Each strain can provide a variety of effects depending on the cannabinoid and terpene content and how they interact with each other.

I, personally, use cannabis to treat chronic pain; inflammation; anxiety; insomnia sciatica; RLS; PMS; and a long list of other ailments.

In addition to relieving what seems like countless symptoms, we all know that cannabis can open our minds and provide us with a variety of thoughts, emotions, and ideas.

Which strains make you euphorically happy? Which strains give you amazing ideas or help you problem solve? Which strains unexpectedly made you too relaxed to function and you want to remember to avoid during certain times of the day?

Common Cannabis Strains

How many have you tried?

Blue Dream	Ghost Train Haze
Pineapple Express	Green Crack
Purple Hindu Kush	Harlequin
Durban Poison	Purple Haze
Girl Scout Cookies	Strawberry Cough
Grape Ape	Super Lemon Haze
Northern Lights	Chocolope
Chernobyl	Sour Diesel
Dutch Treat	Cherry Pie
Mango Kush	Maui Waui
Trainwreck	Cheese
White Widow	Jack Herer

Strains I want to try

_____   _____

_____   _____

_____   _____

_____   _____

_____   _____

_____   _____

_____   _____

_____   _____

_____   _____

_____   _____

_____   _____

_____

Strain: _____

Sativa Indica Hybrid

Date: _____ Time: _____
Lineage of strain: _____

Where Obtianed: _____
Grower: _____Price: _____
Cannabinoid Content: ___%THC ___%CBD ___%
Method used to consume: _____
How much Consumed: _____

Thoughts, feeling, symptoms prior to consumtion:
_____
_____
_____
_____
_____
_____
_____
_____
_____
_____
_____
_____
_____

Thoughts, feelings, symptoms after to consumtion:

_____
_____
_____
_____
_____
_____
_____
_____
_____
_____
_____
_____
_____
_____
_____
_____
_____
_____
_____
_____
_____
_____
_____
_____
_____
_____
_____
_____

Strain: _____

Sativa   Indica   Hybrid

Date: _____ Time: _____
Lineage of strain: _____

Where Obtianed: _____
Grower: _____ Price: _____
Cannabinoid Content: ___%THC ___%CBD ___%
Method used to consume: _____
How much Consumed: _____

Thoughts, feeling, symptoms prior to consumtion:
_____
_____
_____
_____
_____
_____
_____
_____
_____
_____
_____
_____
_____
_____

Thoughts, feelings, symptoms after to consumtion:

_____
_____
_____
_____
_____
_____
_____
_____
_____
_____
_____
_____
_____
_____
_____
_____
_____
_____
_____
_____
_____
_____
_____
_____
_____

Strain: _____

Sativa   Indica   Hybrid

Date: _____ Time: _____

Lineage of strain: _____

Where Obtianed: _____

Grower: _____ Price: _____

Cannabinoid Content: ___%THC ___%CBD ___%

Method used to consume: _____

How much Consumed: _____

Thoughts, feeling, symptoms prior to consumtion:

_____
_____
_____
_____
_____
_____
_____
_____
_____
_____
_____
_____
_____

Thoughts, feelings, symptoms after to consumtion:

_____
_____
_____
_____
_____
_____
_____
_____
_____
_____
_____
_____
_____
_____
_____
_____
_____
_____
_____
_____
_____
_____
_____
_____
_____

Strain: _____

Sativa   Indica   Hybrid

Date: _____ Time: _____
Lineage of strain: _____

Where Obtianed: _____
Grower: _____ Price: _____
Cannabinoid Content: ___%THC ___%CBD ___%
Method used to consume: _____
How much Consumed: _____

Thoughts, feeling, symptoms prior to consumtion:

_____
_____
_____
_____
_____
_____
_____
_____
_____
_____
_____
_____

Thoughts, feelings, symptoms after to consumtion:

_____
_____
_____
_____
_____
_____
_____
_____
_____
_____
_____
_____
_____
_____
_____
_____
_____
_____
_____
_____
_____
_____
_____
_____
_____

Strain: _____

Sativa   Indica   Hybrid

Date: _____ Time: _____
Lineage of strain: _____

Where Obtianed: _____
Grower: _____ Price: _____
Cannabinoid Content: ___%THC ___%CBD ___%
Method used to consume: _____
How much Consumed: _____

Thoughts, feeling, symptoms prior to consumtion:
_____
_____
_____
_____
_____
_____
_____
_____
_____
_____
_____
_____
_____

Thoughts, feelings, symptoms after to consumtion:

_____
_____
_____
_____
_____
_____
_____
_____
_____
_____
_____
_____
_____
_____
_____
_____
_____
_____
_____
_____
_____
_____
_____
_____

Strain: _____

Sativa Indica Hybrid

Date: _____ Time: _____
Lineage of strain: _____

Where Obtianed: _____
Grower: _____ Price: _____
Cannabinoid Content: ___%THC ___%CBD ___%
Method used to consume: _____
How much Consumed: _____

Thoughts, feeling, symptoms prior to consumtion:
_____
_____
_____
_____
_____
_____
_____
_____
_____
_____
_____
_____
_____
_____

Thoughts, feelings, symptoms after to consumtion:

_____
_____
_____
_____
_____
_____
_____
_____
_____
_____
_____
_____
_____
_____
_____
_____
_____
_____
_____
_____
_____
_____
_____
_____
_____

Strain: _____

Sativa   Indica   Hybrid

Date: _____ Time: _____
Lineage of strain: _____

Where Obtianed: _____
Grower: _____Price: _____
Cannabinoid Content: ___%THC ___%CBD ___%
Method used to consume: _____
How much Consumed: _____

Thoughts, feeling, symptoms prior to consumtion:
_____
_____
_____
_____
_____
_____
_____
_____
_____
_____
_____
_____
_____
_____

Thoughts, feelings, symptoms after to consumtion:

_____
_____
_____
_____
_____
_____
_____
_____
_____
_____
_____
_____
_____
_____
_____
_____
_____
_____
_____
_____
_____
_____
_____

Strain: _____
Sativa Indica Hybrid

Date: _____ Time: _____

Lineage of strain: _____

Where Obtianed: _____

Grower: _____Price: _____

Cannabinoid Content: ___%THC ___%CBD ___%

Method used to consume: _____

How much Consumed: _____

Thoughts, feeling, symptoms prior to consumtion:

_____
_____
_____
_____
_____
_____
_____
_____
_____
_____
_____
_____
_____
_____
_____

Thoughts, feelings, symptoms after to consumtion:

_____
_____
_____
_____
_____
_____
_____
_____
_____
_____
_____
_____
_____
_____
_____
_____
_____
_____
_____
_____
_____
_____
_____
_____

Strain: _____

Sativa   Indica   Hybrid

Date: _____ Time: _____
Lineage of strain: _____

Where Obtianed: _____
Grower: _____ Price: _____
Cannabinoid Content: ___%THC ___%CBD ___%
Method used to consume: _____
How much Consumed: _____

Thoughts, feeling, symptoms prior to consumtion:
_____
_____
_____
_____
_____
_____
_____
_____
_____
_____
_____
_____
_____

Thoughts, feelings, symptoms after to consumtion:

_____
_____
_____
_____
_____
_____
_____
_____
_____
_____
_____
_____
_____
_____
_____
_____
_____
_____
_____
_____
_____
_____
_____
_____
_____
_____

Strain: _____

Sativa   Indica   Hybrid

Date: _____ Time: _____
Lineage of strain: _____

Where Obtianed: _____
Grower: _____ Price: _____
Cannabinoid Content: ___%THC ___%CBD ___%
Method used to consume: _____
How much Consumed: _____

Thoughts, feeling, symptoms prior to consumtion:
_____
_____
_____
_____
_____
_____
_____
_____
_____
_____
_____
_____
_____

Thoughts, feelings, symptoms after to consumtion:

_____
_____
_____
_____
_____
_____
_____
_____
_____
_____
_____
_____
_____
_____
_____
_____
_____
_____
_____
_____
_____
_____
_____
_____
_____
_____
_____
_____

Strain: _____

Sativa   Indica   Hybrid

Date: _____ Time: _____
Lineage of strain: _____

Where Obtianed: _____
Grower: _____ Price: _____
Cannabinoid Content: ___%THC ___%CBD ___%
Method used to consume: _____
How much Consumed: _____

Thoughts, feeling, symptoms prior to consumtion:
_____
_____
_____
_____
_____
_____
_____
_____
_____
_____
_____
_____
_____
_____
_____

Thoughts, feelings, symptoms after to consumtion:

_____
_____
_____
_____
_____
_____
_____
_____
_____
_____
_____
_____
_____
_____
_____
_____
_____
_____
_____
_____
_____
_____
_____
_____
_____
_____

Strain: _____

Sativa   Indica   Hybrid

Date: _____ Time: _____
Lineage of strain: _____

Where Obtianed: _____
Grower: _____ Price: _____
Cannabinoid Content: ___%THC ___%CBD ___%
Method used to consume: _____
How much Consumed: _____

Thoughts, feeling, symptoms prior to consumtion:
_____
_____
_____
_____
_____
_____
_____
_____
_____
_____
_____
_____
_____
_____

Thoughts, feelings, symptoms after to consumtion:

_____

_____

_____

_____

_____

_____

_____

_____

_____

_____

_____

_____

_____

_____

_____

_____

_____

_____

_____

_____

_____

_____

_____

_____

_____

_____

Strain: _____

Sativa   Indica   Hybrid

Date: _____ Time: _____
Lineage of strain: _____

Where Obtianed: _____
Grower: _____ Price: _____
Cannabinoid Content: ___%THC ___%CBD ___%
Method used to consume: _____
How much Consumed: _____

Thoughts, feeling, symptoms prior to consumtion:

_____
_____
_____
_____
_____
_____
_____
_____
_____
_____
_____
_____

Thoughts, feelings, symptoms after to consumtion:

_____
_____
_____
_____
_____
_____
_____
_____
_____
_____
_____
_____
_____
_____
_____
_____
_____
_____
_____
_____
_____
_____
_____
_____
_____
_____
_____

Strain: _____

Sativa   Indica   Hybrid

Date: _____ Time: _____

Lineage of strain: _____

Where Obtianed: _____

Grower: _____ Price: _____

Cannabinoid Content: ___%THC ___%CBD ___%

Method used to consume: _____

How much Consumed: _____

Thoughts, feeling, symptoms prior to consumtion:

_____

_____

_____

_____

_____

_____

_____

_____

_____

_____

_____

_____

_____

_____

Thoughts, feelings, symptoms after to consumtion:

_____
_____
_____
_____
_____
_____
_____
_____
_____
_____
_____
_____
_____
_____
_____
_____
_____
_____
_____
_____
_____
_____
_____
_____
_____
_____

Strain: _____

Sativa   Indica   Hybrid

Date: _____ Time: _____
Lineage of strain: _____

Where Obtianed: _____
Grower: _____Price: _____
Cannabinoid Content: ___%THC ___%CBD ___%
Method used to consume: _____
How much Consumed: _____

Thoughts, feeling, symptoms prior to consumtion:

_____
_____
_____
_____
_____
_____
_____
_____
_____
_____
_____
_____
_____

Thoughts, feelings, symptoms after to consumtion:

_____

_____

_____

_____

_____

_____

_____

_____

_____

_____

_____

_____

_____

_____

_____

_____

_____

_____

_____

_____

_____

_____

_____

Strain: _____

Sativa   Indica   Hybrid

Date: _____ Time: _____
Lineage of strain: _____

Where Obtianed: _____
Grower: _____ Price: _____
Cannabinoid Content: ___%THC ___%CBD ___%
Method used to consume: _____
How much Consumed: _____

Thoughts, feeling, symptoms prior to consumtion:
_____
_____
_____
_____
_____
_____
_____
_____
_____
_____
_____
_____
_____
_____

Thoughts, feelings, symptoms after to consumtion:

_____

_____

_____

_____

_____

_____

_____

_____

_____

_____

_____

_____

_____

_____

_____

_____

_____

_____

_____

_____

_____

_____

_____

Strain: _____

Sativa   Indica   Hybrid

Date: _____ Time: _____
Lineage of strain: _____

Where Obtianed: _____
Grower: _____Price: _____
Cannabinoid Content: ___%THC ___%CBD ___%
Method used to consume: _____
How much Consumed: _____

Thoughts, feeling, symptoms prior to consumtion:

_____
_____
_____
_____
_____
_____
_____
_____
_____
_____
_____
_____
_____
_____

Thoughts, feelings, symptoms after to consumtion:

_____
_____
_____
_____
_____
_____
_____
_____
_____
_____
_____
_____
_____
_____
_____
_____
_____
_____
_____
_____
_____
_____
_____

Strain: _____

Sativa   Indica   Hybrid

Date: _____ Time: _____
Lineage of strain: _____

Where Obtianed: _____
Grower: _____Price: _____
Cannabinoid Content: ___%THC ___%CBD ___%
Method used to consume: _____
How much Consumed: _____

Thoughts, feeling, symptoms prior to consumtion:
_____
_____
_____
_____
_____
_____
_____
_____
_____
_____
_____
_____
_____
_____

Thoughts, feelings, symptoms after to consumtion:

_____

_____

_____

_____

_____

_____

_____

_____

_____

_____

_____

_____

_____

_____

_____

_____

_____

_____

_____

_____

_____

_____

_____

_____

_____

_____

Strain: _____
Sativa   Indica   Hybrid

Date: _____ Time: _____
Lineage of strain: _____

Where Obtianed: _____
Grower: _____ Price: _____
Cannabinoid Content: ___%THC ___%CBD ___%
Method used to consume: _____
How much Consumed: _____

Thoughts, feeling, symptoms prior to consumtion:
_____
_____
_____
_____
_____
_____
_____
_____
_____
_____
_____
_____
_____
_____
_____
_____

Thoughts, feelings, symptoms after to consumtion:

_____
_____
_____
_____
_____
_____
_____
_____
_____
_____
_____
_____
_____
_____
_____
_____
_____
_____
_____
_____
_____
_____
_____
_____

Strain: _____

Sativa   Indica   Hybrid

Date: _____ Time: _____

Lineage of strain: _____

Where Obtianed: _____

Grower: _____ Price: _____

Cannabinoid Content: ___%THC ___%CBD ___%

Method used to consume: _____

How much Consumed: _____

Thoughts, feeling, symptoms prior to consumtion:

_____
_____
_____
_____
_____
_____
_____
_____
_____
_____
_____
_____
_____

Thoughts, feelings, symptoms after to consumtion:

_____
_____
_____
_____
_____
_____
_____
_____
_____
_____
_____
_____
_____
_____
_____
_____
_____
_____
_____
_____
_____
_____
_____
_____
_____
_____
_____
_____

Strain: _____

Sativa   Indica   Hybrid

Date: _____ Time: _____

Lineage of strain: _____

Where Obtianed: _____

Grower: _____ Price: _____

Cannabinoid Content: ___%THC ___%CBD ___%

Method used to consume: _____

How much Consumed: _____

Thoughts, feeling, symptoms prior to consumtion:

_____

_____

_____

_____

_____

_____

_____

_____

_____

_____

_____

_____

_____

_____

Thoughts, feelings, symptoms after to consumtion:

_____

_____

_____

_____

_____

_____

_____

_____

_____

_____

_____

_____

_____

_____

_____

_____

_____

_____

_____

_____

_____

_____

_____

_____

_____

Strain: _____

Sativa   Indica   Hybrid

Date: _____ Time: _____
Lineage of strain: _____

Where Obtianed: _____
Grower: _____ Price: _____
Cannabinoid Content: ___%THC ___%CBD ___%
Method used to consume: _____
How much Consumed: _____

Thoughts, feeling, symptoms prior to consumtion:

_____
_____
_____
_____
_____
_____
_____
_____
_____
_____
_____
_____
_____
_____

Thoughts, feelings, symptoms after to consumtion:

_____
_____
_____
_____
_____
_____
_____
_____
_____
_____
_____
_____
_____
_____
_____
_____
_____
_____
_____
_____
_____
_____

Strain: _____

Sativa   Indica   Hybrid

Date: _____ Time: _____
Lineage of strain: _____

Where Obtianed: _____
Grower: _____Price: _____
Cannabinoid Content: ___%THC ___%CBD ___%
Method used to consume: _____
How much Consumed: _____

Thoughts, feeling, symptoms prior to consumtion:
_____
_____
_____
_____
_____
_____
_____
_____
_____
_____
_____
_____
_____
_____

Thoughts, feelings, symptoms after to consumtion:

_____
_____
_____
_____
_____
_____
_____
_____
_____
_____
_____
_____
_____
_____
_____
_____
_____
_____
_____
_____
_____
_____
_____
_____
_____

Strain: _____

Sativa   Indica   Hybrid

Date: _____ Time: _____

Lineage of strain: _____

Where Obtianed: _____

Grower: _____ Price: _____

Cannabinoid Content: ___%THC ___%CBD ___%

Method used to consume: _____

How much Consumed: _____

Thoughts, feeling, symptoms prior to consumtion:

_____
_____
_____
_____
_____
_____
_____
_____
_____
_____
_____
_____
_____
_____

Thoughts, feelings, symptoms after to consumtion:

_____

_____

_____

_____

_____

_____

_____

_____

_____

_____

_____

_____

_____

_____

_____

_____

_____

_____

_____

_____

_____

_____

_____

_____

_____

Strain: _____

Sativa   Indica   Hybrid

Date: _____ Time: _____
Lineage of strain: _____

Where Obtianed: _____
Grower: _____Price: _____
Cannabinoid Content: ___%THC ___%CBD ___%
Method used to consume: _____
How much Consumed: _____

Thoughts, feeling, symptoms prior to consumtion:
_____
_____
_____
_____
_____
_____
_____
_____
_____
_____
_____
_____
_____

Thoughts, feelings, symptoms after to consumtion:

_____
_____
_____
_____
_____
_____
_____
_____
_____
_____
_____
_____
_____
_____
_____
_____
_____
_____
_____
_____
_____
_____
_____
_____
_____
_____

Strain: _____

Sativa   Indica   Hybrid

Date: _____ Time: _____
Lineage of strain: _____

Where Obtianed: _____
Grower: _____ Price: _____
Cannabinoid Content: ___%THC ___%CBD ___%
Method used to consume: _____
How much Consumed: _____

Thoughts, feeling, symptoms prior to consumtion:
_____
_____
_____
_____
_____
_____
_____
_____
_____
_____
_____
_____
_____

Thoughts, feelings, symptoms after to consumtion:

_____
_____
_____
_____
_____
_____
_____
_____
_____
_____
_____
_____
_____
_____
_____
_____
_____
_____
_____
_____
_____
_____
_____

Strain: _____

Sativa   Indica   Hybrid

Date: _____ Time: _____
Lineage of strain: _____

Where Obtianed: _____
Grower: _____Price: _____
Cannabinoid Content: ___%THC ___%CBD ___%
Method used to consume: _____
How much Consumed: _____

Thoughts, feeling, symptoms prior to consumtion:
_____
_____
_____
_____
_____
_____
_____
_____
_____
_____
_____
_____
_____
_____
_____

Thoughts, feelings, symptoms after to consumtion:

_____

_____

_____

_____

_____

_____

_____

_____

_____

_____

_____

_____

_____

_____

_____

_____

_____

_____

_____

_____

_____

_____

_____

_____

_____

Strain: _____

Sativa   Indica   Hybrid

Date: _____ Time: _____
Lineage of strain: _____

Where Obtianed: _____
Grower: _____Price: _____
Cannabinoid Content: ___%THC ___%CBD ___%
Method used to consume: _____
How much Consumed: _____

Thoughts, feeling, symptoms prior to consumtion:

_____
_____
_____
_____
_____
_____
_____
_____
_____
_____
_____
_____
_____

Thoughts, feelings, symptoms after to consumtion:

_____

_____

_____

_____

_____

_____

_____

_____

_____

_____

_____

_____

_____

_____

_____

_____

_____

_____

_____

_____

_____

_____

_____

_____

_____

_____

Strain: _____
Sativa   Indica   Hybrid

Date: _____ Time: _____
Lineage of strain: _____

Where Obtianed: _____
Grower: _____Price: _____
Cannabinoid Content: ___%THC ___%CBD ___%
Method used to consume: _____
How much Consumed: _____

Thoughts, feeling, symptoms prior to consumtion:
_____
_____
_____
_____
_____
_____
_____
_____
_____
_____
_____
_____
_____

Thoughts, feelings, symptoms after to consumtion:

_____
_____
_____
_____
_____
_____
_____
_____
_____
_____
_____
_____
_____
_____
_____
_____
_____
_____
_____
_____
_____
_____
_____
_____
_____

Strain: _____

Sativa   Indica   Hybrid

Date: _____ Time: _____
Lineage of strain: _____

Where Obtianed: _____
Grower: _____Price: _____
Cannabinoid Content: ___%THC ___%CBD ___%
Method used to consume: _____
How much Consumed: _____

Thoughts, feeling, symptoms prior to consumtion:
_____
_____
_____
_____
_____
_____
_____
_____
_____
_____
_____
_____
_____

Thoughts, feelings, symptoms after to consumtion:

_____
_____
_____
_____
_____
_____
_____
_____
_____
_____
_____
_____
_____
_____
_____
_____
_____
_____
_____
_____
_____
_____
_____
_____
_____

Strain: _____

Sativa Indica Hybrid

Date: _____ Time: _____

Lineage of strain: _____

Where Obtianed: _____

Grower: _____Price: _____

Cannabinoid Content: ___%THC ___%CBD ___%

Method used to consume: _____

How much Consumed: _____

Thoughts, feeling, symptoms prior to consumtion:

_____

_____

_____

_____

_____

_____

_____

_____

_____

_____

_____

_____

_____

_____

Thoughts, feelings, symptoms after to consumtion:

_____

_____

_____

_____

_____

_____

_____

_____

_____

_____

_____

_____

_____

_____

_____

_____

_____

_____

_____

_____

_____

_____

_____

_____

_____

_____

_____

_____